COTSWOLD COUN

Centred on the gentle slopes … this beautiful area is famo… …ges, many scarcely altered … …ity of the medieval woo… …e Cotswolds lies in Glouc… …es into Worcestershire and Oxfo… …nce given over almost entirely to sheep-fa… …ny of the fine churches and manor-houses owe the… existence to the generosity of wealthy 14th and 15th century yeoman farmers and wool merchants. The dignified villages gain much of their charm from the use of the warm, honey-coloured limestone which was locally quarried and used alike for humble cottages, mansions and churches. Never far from sight, numerous streams wind through the valleys and chatter alongside main streets.

Bourton-on-the-Water is often referred to as the Venice of the Cotswolds on account of the bridges spanning the crystal clear waters of the River Windrush, which passes through the village. The river is flanked by broad grass verges and two of the bridges date from the 18th century. Sights of the village include the Model Village, an exact $\frac{1}{9}$th size replica of the village, the Old Mill Motor Museum and Birdland.

The little River Eye links the villages of Upper and Lower Slaughter which are among the loveliest spots in the Cotswolds. In **Lower Slaughter**, the stream meanders through the centre of the village crossed by several low foot-bridges. Nearby stands an early 19th century corn mill which was still working in the 1960s. **Upper Slaughter** has grown up a mile away, on a gentle grassy slope above the little brook. Once the village was dominated by a Norman castle but all that can be seen of it today are the remains of the motte and bailey.

Lower Slaughter

Manor House, Upper Slaughter

With its long line of dormer windows, the beautiful gabled Manor House at Upper Slaughter is one of the finest buildings in the area. The oldest part of the house dates from the 15th century but the front is Elizabethan.

The fine Norman church in Upper Slaughter has some outstanding features. A splendid arch leads into the church from the tower with some exceptionally well - preserved moulding. Some fragments of ancient carving can be seen in the wall of the church which, unusually, contains two fonts – one 15th century and one a modern replica.

Stow-on-the-Wold from the church tower

The Square and Cross, Stow-on-the-Wold

Stow-on-the-Wold stands exposed on a 700 feet high hill at the junction of seven major roads, including the Roman Fosse Way. At the height of the Cotswold wool industry the town was famous for its huge annual fairs where as many as 20,000 sheep were sold at one time. The vast Market Square testifies to the town's former importance. At one end stands the ancient cross, and at the other the town stocks, shaded beneath an old elm tree.

Surrounded by the gentle scenery of the Upper Winrush Valley, **Naunton** is a delightful village of golden buildings offset by green fields and dark trees. Consisting of a single main street, it is one of the most peaceful of the villages in the northern Cotswolds. Standing by the river, Naunton's restored church has more than 500 years of recorded history and contains some interesting monuments as well as a fine pulpit of white stone. All that remains of the manor house is a large dovecot containing almost 2000 nesting boxes.

Naunton

Guiting Power

Guiting Power is a delightful old village where a fascinating variety of cottages cluster around a gently-sloping, triangular green. The church, thoughtfully restored in the early 1900s, has a fine 15th century roof and two splendid Norman doorways. About two miles north of the village is the **Cotswold Farm Park**, a rare breed survival centre. Established in 1970 at Bemborough Farm, a typical working Cotswold farm, the centre provides an environment where rare breeds of farm animal can live and breed in natural surroundings. Among many varieties of sheep and cattle which are preserved here are West Highland and Longhorn cattle and the distinctive Cotswold Lions. These heavily fleeced sheep were once numerous throughout the area but were threatened with extinction by the decline of the Cotswold wool trade.

Sudeley Castle has a varied and interesting history. Re-built in the 15th century, it was later owned by Sir Thomas Seymour who married Henry VIII's widow, Catherine Parr. She is buried in the chapel, one of the few parts of the original building to survive. Later restored as a manor house, Sudeley Castle stands in delightful gardens.

Winchcombe, nestling in a wooded valley on the north-western edge of the Cotswolds, is a pleasing small town with a history dating back over 1000 years. In Saxon times it was a town of some importance and once boasted a great abbey. Today it is a quiet little place with many charming cottages such as those which line picturesque Vineyard Street. The fine 15th century parish church has a number of particularly grotesque gargoyles and a fine altar cloth, part of which is said to have been embroidered by Henry VIII's first wife, Katharine of Aragon.

Vineyard Street, Winchcombe

Snowshill *(above)* is a secluded village where pretty cottages and a 19th century church cluster around a small green, Snowshill Manor is a Tudor mansion which contains an interesting collection of clocks, toys and musical instruments. **Stanway** *(below)* is so called because the ancient Stane Way passed through it. The impressive gabled gatehouse to Stanway House is said to have been designed by Inigo Jones.

Stanton is one of the prettiest of the villages which lie around the northern edge of the Cotswolds. Apparently little changed in three hundred years, it nestles beneath the slopes of Shenbarrow Hill. It has a pleasing long main street and there are several delightful corners where the ancient houses are built in typical Cotswold style with steeply-pitched gables, mullioned casements and glowing stone walls. The village contains a number of 16th and 17th century houses as well as a restored, medieval cross and a church in which some Norman work has survived. Nearby Stanton Court is a Jacobean mansion standing in attractive gardens which are sometimes open to the public.

Cottages at Stanton

Snowshill Manor

Broadway Tower

Broadway Tower is a fortress-like folly which overlooks the village from its position on top of 1,024 feet high Broadway Beacon. At the end of the 18th century the ground belonged to the Earl of Coventry and it is said that the Countess persuaded her husband to build the tower which could be seen from the family seat near Worcester. From the top there are magnificent views in all directions which encompass not only the Cotswold Hills but also the lovely Vale of Evesham, the distant ridge of the Malverns and the Forest of Dean.

15th Century Cottages at Broadway

Broadway is one of the showpieces of the Cotswolds and, with its rows of beautiful old stone cottages, it retains a particular charm. The art of Cotswold building is seen at its best in the outstanding group of 15th century cottages at Bankside. In the centre of the village is the green and the Lygon Arms where King Charles I and Oliver Cromwell both stayed. At the eastern end of the village the road zig-zags steeply up Fish Hill to the Fish Inn.

On the northern edge of the Cotswolds surrounded by wooded countryside and winding lanes is secluded **Hidcote Bartrim** *(above)*. The hamlet has some delightful thatched cottages but it is best known for the famous gardens at Hidcote Manor. Created by horticulturalist Major Lawrence Johnston, the gardens comprise a series of delightful small areas surrounded by walls or variegated hedges and each devoted to one species or colour combination.

Hidcote Manor, three miles north of Chipping Campden, is a late 17th century mansion most noted for its attractive informal gardens. Amongst the finest in England they were created this century by the great horticulturalist Major Lawrence Johnston. Famous for their many rare plants and shrubs, the gardens are divided into a number of small areas separated by walls and hedges of great variety.

Blockley *(bottom left)* is a bustling little village which lies in a leafy valley between Chipping Campden and Bourton-on-the-Hill. Its charming stone cottages, many of which were originally home to mill-workers, are clustered around the millpond. Nearby is the handsome church, the tower of which was rebuilt after a great storm in 1703. To the north-west of Blockley is **Willersey**, another typical Cotswold village. The picturesque Bell Inn, the restored Early-English church and a cluster of cottages by the green all combine to give the village its timeless character.

Willersey

Chipping Campden is often described as having the most perfect high street in England with its beautiful stone houses dating from the 14th to the 18th century. In the middle of the street is the 17th century Market Hall. Close by is Grevel's House, built in 1380 by the local merchant William Grevel. The 15th century Parish Church of St James has a graceful interior, containing medieval altar hangings and some fine monumental brasses.

St. James's Church, Chipping Campden

Cottages at Chipping Campden

Bourton-on-the-Hill (*above*) straggles along its steep main street and the pretty cottage gardens are one of the features of the village. The neat little church is medieval, and nearby Bourton House is 16th century with a fine tithe barn. **Chastleton House** (*below*), built around 1603 by rich wool merchant Walter Jones, has remained largely unaltered since the 17th century. The interior displays furniture, ornate carved panelling and fine tapestries and glass.

Moreton-in-Marsh is a small but busy market town at the edge of the northern Cotswolds. Indeed it may have derived its name from its position close to the 'march' or boundary between the counties of Gloucestershire and Oxfordshire. Two miles from the town stands the well-known Four Shire Stone which marks the place where four counties once met. Moreton grew up along the line of the Roman Fosse Way which runs along the wide main street. In isolation in the middle of the street stands the handsome Market Hall which is also known as the Redesdale Hall and was donated to the town in 1951 by Lord Dulverton. Near to the market Hall is the Curfew Tower which houses the original curfew bell which rang every night up to 1860. There is a spacious air about Moreton's tree-lined streets with their attractive old houses and inns.

The Market Hall, Moreton-in-Marsh

Market day at Moreton-in-Marsh

Woodstock is a pretty market town to the north of Oxford. It boasts many charming streets and in Park Street *(above)* stands the historic Bear Hotel and the medieval stocks. Close to the town is the magnificent 18th century **Blenheim Palace** *(below)*, set in a vast park. Built by Sir John Vanburgh it was a gift from the nation to the 1st Duke of Marlborough in recognition of his victories over the French.

Chipping Norton *(above)* is one of the north-eastern outposts of Cotswold architecture. The centre of the town is the market place with its classical style Town Hall. The Parish Church has an unusual two-storied hexagonal porch. **The Rollright Stones** *(below)* lie between the villages of Great and Little Rollright to the north of Chipping Norton. There are two sets of stones known as the "Circle" and the "Whispering Knights".

Witney is a bustling little town on the edge of the Cotswolds. The weaving of woollen cloth is believed to have begun here in Roman times and Witney became famous for the production of fine blankets. Standing on the banks of the River Leach, the hamlet of **Eastleach Martin** dates from Norman times. The church of St. Michael and St. Martin boasts five ancient sundials and contains some beautiful Norman and 14th century work.

High Street, Burford

In the days of the Wychwood Fair, the **Shaven Crown Inn** was a scene of bustle and excitement. Now, carefully preserved, this lovely old building with its fine Tudor gateway is peacefully situated in the quiet little village of Shipton-under-Wychwood.

Shaven Crown Inn

Lamb Inn, Burford

The beautiful old town of **Burford** on the River Windrush was the site of a fortified ford in Anglo-Saxon times. The town grew to be an important crossroads and busy wool town and today it is a popular centre for visitors. The broad main street slopes gently down to the river, lined with dignified old houses and shops, many of which appear little changed since Tudor times. The Lamb Inn is one of the most charming of the numerous old coaching inns which testify to Burford's importance over the years.

The small town of **Northleach** comprises a pleasant collection of houses and cottages around a main square. The fine Perpendicular church is seen to advantage across the fields and contains a number of notable brasses. **Fairford** lies beside the River Coln a little downstream of Bibury. The village has a picturesque old water mill, and a magnificent 'wool' church with an unrivalled collection of 15th century stained glass.

Midway between Cirencester and Bibury is the pretty little village of Barnsley with its ancient church and attractive dormer-windowed cottages. **Barnsley House** is a fine late-Renaissance house famous principally as the home of a considerable collection of books once owned by Sir Isaac Newton. The philosopher and scientist had no personal connection with Barnsley and the preservation of some 800 to 900 of his books is due to one of his biographers, Colonel de Villamil. Situated where four counties come together, **Lechlade** in Gloucestershire is a fine Georgian market town. St. John's Lock is the first lock on the River Thames and near here the River Leach, from which the town gets its name, joins the Thames as it meanders through the grazing meadows.

Barnsley House and Garden

St. John's Lock, Lechlade

Arlington Row, Bibury

Cottages at Bibury

The 19th century artist and poet William Morris called **Bibury** "the most beautiful village in England". Nestling in the valley of the River Coln, it is certainly one of the most perfect spots in the Cotswolds. The delightful terrace known as Arlington Row was originally built as a sheep-house in the 14th century. It was converted in the 1600s to provide cottages for the weavers who supplied cloth to nearby Arlington Mill. This splendid 17th century corn mill, which was restored and enlarged in 1859, was at one time also used for fulling – the process by which newly woven cloth is cleaned and thickened. Some machinery can be seen in operation in the mill which also contains an interesting folk museum. The mill-stream flows past Arlington Row to join the slow-moving River Coln as it winds between wooded banks. Near the Swan Inn the river, a celebrated haunt of trout fishermen, is spanned by a fine old road bridge which dates from 1770.

Arlington Row, Bibury

River Coln and The Swan Inn

The Parish Church, Cirencester

Cirencester is one of England's most ancient towns. It was known to the Romans as Corinium and was at that time the second largest city in Britain after London. Many Roman relics have been discovered including floor mosaics and a large amphitheatre. Dominating the market place is the 15th century Church of St. John the Baptist which was built when Cirencester was the most important wool market in England. The church has some exquisite stonework, notably the elaborate tracery on the three-storey south porch. It is also noted for its soaring west tower and magnificent nave.

The village of **Minchinhampton** has an unusual parish church and a fine Market Hall dating from 1698. To the north are Minchinhampton and Rodborough Commons, which offer excellent walks and fine views.

The famous **Westonbirt Arboretum** is one of the finest tree collections in the country. Situated about three miles south-west of Tetbury, it was founded in 1829 and is now managed by the Foresty Commission. Particularly beautiful in autumn, it is also a blaze of colour earlier in the year when banks of rhododendrons are in flower.

Open commons and steep-sided valleys characterise the area around Stroud and from **Rodborough Common** *(above)* there are fine views of the Gloucestershire countryside. The castellated mansion known as Rodborough Fort is a distinctive local landmark. **Painswick** *(below)* sometimes called "Queen of the Cotswolds", has many quaint corners. The churchyard is famous for its clipped yew trees some of which are over 200 years old.

Cheltenham is an inland spa resort of handsome Regency architecture, broad avenues and fine parks. It owed its development to the discovery, in the 1730's, of medicinal waters which can be taken at several sites in the town, mainly the Pittville Pump Room. Principal street of Cheltenham is the Promenade with its fine Regency terraces and Neptune Fountain. South of the town is the distinctive rock formation known as The Devil's Chimney.